Changing Faces

An Epic Journey From Gangsta To Gospel Rapper

By

Monique Flanagan

Aka: **"Sista Monique"**

Changing Faces

An Epic Journey From Gangsta To Gospel Rapper

By:

Monique Flanagan

Published By:

ABM Publications

A division of Andrew Bills Ministries, Inc.
PO Box 6811, Orange, CA 92863
www.abmpublications.com

ISBN: 978-1-931820-54-7

SPECIAL DEDICATION & ACKNOWLEDGEMENTS

With everything I am, I give special thanks to my Lord and Savior Jesus Christ. Man, all those times I had a gun to my head and you saved me, all those times I turned my back on you, and yet you still saved me. Thanks you for my Born-Again life. Jesus, you saved me. I love you so much, my Lord. All thanks to you for saving me.

Thanks to everyone who had a part of the group Female Assassins. It was a pleasure working with you all, but God hit me up when He knew I was ready for this Gospel journey.

Thanks to all the ministers God sent my way, and I'm sorry for being a knuckle-head. Thanks to my Pastor Sam Sellers and Evangelist Renae Sellers; thanks for pushing me, believing in me and never giving up on me.

Thanks to my boys, Domonique and Malique Flanagan. Mommy loves you guys.

Most of all, thanks to the readers of this book. I love you.....

Sista Monique

TABLE OF CONTENTS

OPENING PRAYER

Father God, I love you and I never want to leave Your Presence for I'm nothing without you. Father, I thank you for this opportunity to influence others to give their lives to Christ and to learn to forgive. I want to inspire and impact the readers of this book. I want my brothers and sisters to be empowered through your grace, which is how we all conquer every giant obstacle that comes our way.

I want the readers to know that even if they were physically, mentally or verbally abused, abandoned or molested, or even went through the trauma of rape, it is possible to learn to forgive. They can know that we are each loved and that we are somebody, and WE are VICTORIOUS in Christ!!!!!.

In Jesus name, Amen.

INTRODUCTION

My name is Monique Latrice (Trice) Flanagan. I was born February 7, 1972 in the city of Flint, Michigan. I'm the oldest child of nine, and I am the mother of two children of my own.

This book does not contain the story of my whole life, but there are certain areas that I wanted to write about and put in this book. Some names have been changed.

I pray that you will understand that some of the mean actions came from a mad young lady. I thank God that He has changed me.

I am Born-Again, and I hope you enjoy this book.

MONIQUE FLANAGAN

Chapter 1

A LITTLE HISTORY

To get a better understanding of me, I want to give you a little history. My story starts with my grandmother. Her named was Maeva Cooper Flanagan; she was a very strong woman. I looked up to her; I loved her strength and feistiness. Grandma was the mother of six, she was tall and skinny, knocked-kneed, and she had scars on her legs, thighs, back, and neck. She was a survivor of a horrific domestic dispute. My grandmother's boyfriend at the time pulled out a knife in the middle of one of their fights and began to stab her all over her body, including slicing her neck from ear to ear, leaving her no choice but to run and jump out of a two story window landing on top of a car.

Grandma died three times that night during surgery, and each time she came back fighting; she survived that terrible ordeal. My grandmother was a heavy drinker, some people had labeled her an alcoholic, but I labeled her as someone who didn't take any crap from no one, drunk or sober. I remember our family and friends meeting at my grandma's house every weekend. They drank, played cards and listened to a little music. My grandmother and her boyfriend were owners of a 12 gage rifle. Whenever Grandma got mad at someone, she would run to her room and grab this rifle and everybody would take off running. My little brother and sister and I would sit there and laugh. I know you would think we would be scared, but we were used to it. What we couldn't figure out is, why did people make her mad knowing she was going to get that rifle? It was a repeated offense and it happened all the time!

On the good side, nobody got hurt. But one night my grandmother was walking home from the club, and a man jumped from behind a bush and tried to rape her. Being the fighter she was, she beat the man with one hand and held up her pants with the other hand, and, of course, the man gave up and took off running. She beat the mess out of him. He was lucky he was gone by the time she made it in the house, or she would have gotten a gun and probably would have shot him. She was quite a fighter!

I took it hard the day she stopped fighting, the day she died was March 6, 1997. Just like my grandmother, when people hurt me or crossed me, I wanted to do whatever it takes to get them back. But due to justice being served in some cases, my justice was not done, so at the time I was forced to put my pain and anger on paper and rap about it. I mean, I wrote scary gruesome raps; raps that a producer of a scary movie would have paid for. Now that I'm grown, I know my life wasn't a rap, it was a testimony and my Lord brought me through it all.

Chapter 2

MY BROTHER'S KEEPER

My story started at a very young age. My mom started dating a man when she was pregnant with me. He was very abusive and a heavy drug user. He would get high and beat my mom almost every day of their relationship. One day I was walking up the steps, and I could hear gagging sounds, as I got to the top of the steps I could see this man on top of my mom choking her to death, her tongue was hanging out of her mouth and her eyes were rolled into the back of her head. He turned to me and yelled for me to leave. As I just sat on the steps, rocking back and forward, I was waiting for her to fight back, or waiting to see if he was going to kill her. I often asked myself, "Why won't she hit him back?" I would rather die trying than to let my abuser get control of whether he thought I should die or live.

I was told that when I was two years old, I was crying and he picked me up and threw me and I landed in a chair that had a nail sticking out of it, missing it by an inch. My aunt jumped on him. I knew my mom wouldn't stand up for herself, but what about me?

I received beatings off and on, but on this occasion I remember it was when I was six years old and by this time my mom had two children from him. My little brother was a year younger than me; we got into a fight, and I beat my brother up. His dad, who was watching us from a window, came outside and made us fight again, and I beat my brother again. He smacked my brother and said he better whip me and that I better not hit my brother back. He threw us together like we were in a dogfight. My brother and I were rolling all over that ground; he was determined to win, and I was determined not to lose. I beat the mess out of him. He told my brother "Boys are not supposed to let girls beat them" and he told me, "Girls are not supposed to fight back." He made us fight again, and I won again.

I'm not my mother; I will fight back, by all means necessary. (And that's what I learned from my grandmother.) My brother's father took me in the house and beat me with an extension cord, he beat me for standing my ground, he beat me for not being my mother, he beat me for all the men who think women are not supposed to hit back, he beat me bloody. All I could do was scream out for help, scream for my mom, who was too afraid to move. At that time I hated my mom, I wanted to love her, she needed my love, but I needed her protection. At times I hated my aunties, my dad, I hated everybody. I thought "What's wrong with me? Why didn't anybody save me? Why didn't anybody stop the abuse?" All those grownups did nothing."

I don't know how I knew there was a God, but I felt His Presence and I would often look in the sky and talk to Him. "Please get me away from these people." See we were not raised in the church, nobody was talking about God, we were learning how to play cards and shoot dice. But I talked to Him every day. I knew my grandmother would have gotten me if she could, but the way she drank, there is no way the system would let her get me. One day I remembered that I made my mom mad, and she blurted out that's why I was a rape baby. She said that her and my dad had broken up, and he called and asked if he could come and talk to her. She said after she had opened the door that he began to throw himself on her and assaulted her. When she told me this story, that's when I knew I was special, I might have been a mistake, but God had a plan for me. This began to develop my testimony.

Chapter 3

GOT TALENT

The mid 80's is when I discovered I had a talent for rapping. It was when my favorite movie came out "Crush Groove". They say Blondie was the first female rapper, some even say it was Salt and Pepa. And maybe it was, I could have been late in the game. But the first female I saw rap was Shelia E, in the movie Crush Groove, and I knew it was something I could do. After I had turned a poem into a rap, it was on and poppin'. Another girl and I had formed a rap group called the Deff Dames.

We thought we were the best thing that ever hit the rap game, we did a couple of talent shows, a couple of rap battles, but we didn't last long. With our different life styles, Shonda was a straight A student, and she had to study a lot, her mom was strict on her and she couldn't do as much as I could. I was free will, and I did what I wanted when I wanted. But breaking us up didn't stop me, that was a whole new life for me.

Rap was something I could take my anger out on and boy did I release some anger.

Chapter 4

ANGRY SOUL

My mom had four sisters and one brother; he was my Uncle Roscoe. He was rough with us whenever he would come around. He would make us sing and dance, he would put on a show and my cousin and I were his backup singers.

One day my friend Mary and I went to go visit my cousin, and my uncle came over. He was in his playing mood, and he was rough. See the thing of this is we were used to it, but my friend wasn't used to that. My friend told me she was ready to go home, and I was going to walk her home, but my uncle wouldn't stop. I asked him to stop, and he hit me, this was not the playful hit, this was serious. When he hit me, I started hitting him back, and we wrestled all over my auntie's house. My uncle was hitting me like I was a man in the streets. So when I got to my feet, I ran and grabbed a knife and stabbed him. He went into a rage and said he was going to kill me, but I thought "not if I kill him first." All I could think about was my sister and brother's dad. My uncle was not my uncle any more, in my mind he was my brother's daddy.

I was not my mother, and I was old enough to defend myself, that's all I knew. I was over-protective of myself. At least I loved me and I was going to stand up for me. I didn't care who it was; nobody was going to just hit me and get away with it.

I left my aunt's house and ran to a neighbor's where my mom was at and told her she better go get her brother and that I had stabbed him. My uncle went to the hospital and stayed for a week or so. Now I knew I cut him, but I didn't think it was that bad.

One day I was walking up to my grandmother's house, and my uncle came out the house walking up to me real fast, Lord I thought we were going to have to fight again. But he gave me fifty dollars and told me "Thanks" because when I cut him and he went to the hospital is when he found out he was sick and didn't know it. They said he came to the hospital at the right time. Now don't get me wrong, I love my uncle and didn't want to hurt him. I just wish people would keep their hands off me. Stop hitting on me. My uncle died a few years after that; I took it hard; I will always miss my uncle.

Chapter 5

LOOKING DOWN THE BARREL

The first time I stared down the barrel of a gun was right after I called my cousin and told her that her boyfriend was trying to talk to one of my friends. My cousin called me the next day and asked if I could come over. As I walked in her house, her boyfriend went right off and said I was lying, and he began to beat me in my head with a bottle. When I fell to the floor, he began to kick and stomp me in my head.

I remembered my mom's beating and remembered my brother's father, I knew I had to get off that floor. He was going to have to kill me, because I knew if I got to my feet, I would fight back. I was slipping and sliding in my very own blood, but I was determined to die trying; it was in my will.

I got to the drawer and got a knife, I swung that knife in every direction I could. I couldn't see because of the blood. I was not going to stop swinging until my last breath.

By time, my friends heard us as they were walking up, so they came running in the house, and he went into another room, so they were trying to help me out the door. When he came back, he pointed a gun in my face. I was not scared because if he killed me, I knew in my heart I died fighting for my life, so I was not going to give up.

One of my friends who was pregnant jumped directly in front of the gun, and the other friend got behind me, they sandwiched me out of the house. If he had shot that gun, he would have shot all three of us.... But GOD; for I knew it was God, that saved us that day. I thank my friends and I will always love them for what they did for me. I never had anyone protect me like that. I'm giving God the Glory. My cousin had moved out of town, and it was nothing I could do but put it on paper.

Chapter 6

THE NAKED MAN

This story is scary and funny both at the same time. In the heart of Flint Michigan, the streets were terrorized, and the women were terrified. There were men breaking into women's houses and raping them in front of their children. But this one man was not one of those that were breaking in or raping.

I don't know what his problem was, but you could be sitting in the house and hear a little tapping on the window or door, and as you began to answer, saying "Who is it?" He wouldn't answer. Then, as you would go look out the window or door, he would be standing there naked and relieving himself out your window or door.

He would have a black T-shirt over his head with the eye's cut out!

One night my friend and I had been drinking, and we were walking through the parking lot of our apartment complex, laughing and talking loud. A girl with long hair was walking in front of the cars, just as we were behind the cars. We spoke to her, "What are you doing out this late?" She didn't speak back, so we thought "Oh well" and we continued talking. My friend asked me, "What if we see The Naked Man?" I got to talking loud, saying what I would do to him if we did see him. I can fight, I'm one woman he doesn't want to mess with.

Well, as we get to the end of the last car, we met up with the girl, and when we got close up on each other, it wasn't a girl. It was The Naked Man!

My big bad tail took off faster than a speeding bullet, screaming and crying. All that crap I just talked, and I know he heard me. I went from Barry White to Michael Jackson, all in one take. He caught me off guard, and I was not ready for that!

He didn't chase us, because he probably was laughing at me and my big mouth. I was supposed to been knocking him out, well that's what I was thinking. I went from a pit bull to a poodle in 2 point 2 seconds!

As for The Naked Man, he ran off into the night. He would often get caught, but they would only charge him with indecent exposure. Glory to God no one got hurt!

Chapter 7

A PREACHER'S PRAYER

After that my family and I had moved to the north side of town. I had enrolled into The Kennedy Center, which was a school known for "The bad and rebellious". This is a school of hard core types, where you had to embrace the motto "Never let them see you sweat".

The first day of school went by fast. On my walk home I met up with a young lady that I went to middle school with, she and I both were new to this school and we had befriended each other. We began to have our weekend "sleep overs" to hang out.

This was the point of my life when I started drinking heavily. Well, this particular weekend was different; when I got to her house she asked me did I want to go with her over to her sister's house. On our way to her sister's house, we stopped by a store and got drinks.

In my head, I thought it was strange that her sister wanted to socialize and drink with teens because when she introduced me to her husband, she said he was a Pastor. He was a Pastor, who had been praying for his wife to stop drinking. I could hear them arguing every time she left the room. But she didn't care and that didn't stop her. Every time she went to the restroom he was right in her face. But she always returned with a smile as if nothing happened. The last time she walked from the table, she said, "Excuse me, I have to go tuck my kids into bed and say our prayers." That caught my attention because no matter how drunk she was she made time for her babies.

I never had that, so I was enjoying being around a mother's love. I could hear her and the kids laughing, talking and praying. I also overheard the Preacher's prayer: he said, "Father, I love you and forgive me for my sins, please forgive me for what I'm about to do."

I heard a loud bang and I saw a bright flash. The kids started screaming and crying; then it got real quiet. The woman walked to the doorway of the kitchen; she was covered in blood, and then she collapsed. I'm looking at this woman who was happy a few minutes ago; now she's lying in a big puddle of blood.

When I lifted my head, I was staring down the barrel of a rifle. He said, "I will kill you if you don't leave my house now!" I ran out the back door and was trapped in the garage, he chased me around an old car, and I had nowhere else to run. He was shouting at me and aiming the gun at me. I then ran back into the house. I could hear his footsteps right behind me, and I heard him cock the rifle. All I could do is run and pray (never looking back). I snatched up my friend, who was drunk and so busy on the phone that she missed the whole thing!

As we were running toward the door, we had to jump over her sister's body. My friend was now crying and asking me what happened. By that time I was out the door and on my way down the street, she was not too far behind me. We made it to the corner store, where the police were called.

Chapter 8

FEMALE ASSASSINS

After that long weekend, it was now Monday and back to school as usual. I was by myself, but it didn't matter to me because there was nothing compared to what I just went through. As I was walking down the hall, some people came up to me asking me if I could rap, and there was this girl who wanted to battle me.

Of course, I was down for a battle. As I walked outside, the whole school was out there. As soon as the young lady stepped out the door, she started flowing on me. When she got done with her rap, all her fans were screaming and giving her high fives. Now, not knowing what I just went through over the weekend with the preacher, I wrote a rap, and in the rap I talked about every gun you could possibly name; because my brother had a gun book.

I also talked about how and who I was going to kill with these guns. Back then, there wasn't too many female rappers and definitely not talking about killing.

I won that battle and then another young lady

wanted to battle me, she was on my level, but little did she know I had a second verse, and it was more hard core then the first verse.

I totally focused on my mother's beating, the preacher and his wife, and my beatings from my brother's father. While I suddenly felt like I was ready to kill, all I could do was rap about it. I rapped so strongly, I also won that battle, but that young lady got offended and wanted to fight. But one of her friends got between us and said we should become a crew, so both agreed.

Now, I don't know how this young man got my phone number, but he called me later on that night and said he heard me rap and that it was the hardest rap he ever heard. He said, "You should call yourself Lady Assassins, and if you ever join a group you should name it the Female Assassins."

The next day at school people was patting me on the back, as my new rap partner Dee walked up with her group of friends, I told her we should call ourselves the Female Assassins. I end up moving in with these young ladies, Qu, Dee, and Low (we was a hit).

We rapped at all the local clubs: T's, Hammer Dropper's and Dendy Boys, just to name a few. We were popular, and the streets of Flint Michigan knew who we were, winning battle after battle. One day Low and I were out rapping to a group of kids on a basketball court. We had just put our guns in the house, thinking we didn't need them around harmless children. Suddenly a grey car came riding up and down the road and when it finally came to a stop, we heard a loud pop, and then it sped off into the night.

I thought it was a firecracker, but as my friend Low said we should go to the house, I felt a pain in my leg. I told her "I think I got shot." My friend thought I was playing, so we started back to walking. I knew I was hit, but I wasn't sure. When we got to the house, I went into the kitchen and pulled down my pants. Lord, when I saw all that flesh and blood on my pants leg, I panicked. I'm screaming and crying, falling out. It's funny now how I walked home and was fine, but the sight of blood and torn flesh threw me into overdrive (pain is a mind-over-matter thing).

I don't know how that bullet bypassed those kids and hit me, but it did and everything happens for a reason. I was shot in the buttocks, it ricocheted off my hip bone and came out the side of my leg. After all those times I've had a gun pulled on me, I ended up getting hit this time. I believed it was God's way of telling me to slow down.

Chapter 9

INTRODUCED TO THE HOLY SPIRIT

I knew of Jesus, but I didn't know Him and His works, what He has done for us and how important it means to have Him in our lives. My younger sister, Nikki's father, had given his life to the Lord, and he would often try to minister to us when he visited with my sister. But being a hard-headed teen, I heard him but I wasn't listening.

After a while, I moved to Waycross Georgia with my aunt, who was deeply involved in the church. This is the point in my life where I got to know God; I got to know Jesus. At my aunt's church, they were speaking in tongues, singing, dancing and shouting, really enjoying the Lord's Spirit. I had never felt this way before, and it felt good. See, my mom never took us to church before unless it was a funeral.

Now I'm 19 years old, and I'm at this church finding my own connection with the Lord. But I still had the urge to rap, so my cousin and I teamed up with brothers who played the drums and the keyboard. We became the Flanagan Girls. Monique and Nichole Flanagan; we did plays; we did it all as long it was dealing with Christ. I was happy, but I missed Michigan, and the temptation of that street life had the best of me, so I moved back home to Flint.

Chapter 10

THE GIRL THEY THOUGHT WAS ME

Home Sweet Home. After teaming back up with my old crew and getting back with my neighborhood friends we all went out to the club this one night. All through the night I was messing with this girl that I didn't like. I would bump into her, knock her drink all over her, step on her feet (just being a bully) This girl was the jack of all trades and I did not like her. She had befriended my friend Tay; they were cool. She would come and visit, and we would all drink together, laugh, talk, and chill.

I had a feeling that she was sleeping with Tay's man. I did not like that at all. Well, after running into this girl at the club and me messing with her all night, I went and sat down at my table, still watching her the whole night. My eyes suddenly caught this guy who was going down the stairs in the basement (where the pool tables were), so I followed him. It was like about 10 minutes into our conversation, we heard noises upstairs as if it was a stampede.

When I made it to the top of the steps, I could see my brother's best friend screaming and crying, rubbing his head. I ran over to him asking him what happened. He looked at me as if he seen a ghost. He grabbed me and said, "Your brother is going crazy, they said you just got shot." I told him I was downstairs in the basement. He said that the girl I'd been messing with was looking for me with a gun and came outside and shot me.

My brother came running back into the club, rushing, grabbing and pulling on me. He said, "People keep saying that you got shot. The girl you was messing with the whole night just shot two people, and I thought you was one of them."

With my brother and his friend running with me, we ran outside where there was a group of people standing around a girl laying on the ground. As I was running past this young lady, they thought was me, my heart went out to her. I wished I hadn't gone out that night; I wished I had not been picking a fight. That night that young lady they thought was me died. My heart felt broken, because I was so sorry for what happened to her.

Chapter 11

MOTHER MAY I

My mom was now out the closet doing drugs again, and she'd been doing drugs with her fourth baby's daddy. This man was just as bad as my brother's daddy because he beat my mom every chance he could, even beating her while she slept.

One day my sister and I went to visit my mom. When we got there, a young white boy answered the door. We walked in the house and of course we gave him the third degree, asking him who was he and where did he come from?

This young man was a mess; he said that he paid my mom with some drugs to stay there, making her house his trap (drug house). With a real rough attitude, he told me and my sister that he ran that house, and it's now his house and he could put us out if he wanted to. Oh well, you know my sister and I gave him the business.

I jacked that little boy up and threw him out the house. The boy ran crying and said he will be back.

After having some words with my mom, I went to the restroom. As I'm on the toilet, I could hear loud banging on the door, and I heard a man's voice saying who is Trice and where is Trice at?

I could hear my mom say, "she's in the bathroom." I was furious, I ran out the bathroom ready for war, and then he and I came face to face. Being me, I was not backing down for nothing. He's in my face telling me to shut up, I'm telling him, "You make me, I'm not an ordinary woman, and I will rock and roll with you." He said, "This is my house, and I pay the rent!" Then I was ready to fight. I told him I would drag him; he called me out my name and I said for him to shut up.

As I'm standing my ground ready to rumble, my sister was behind the man, signing for me to be quiet. But no man was going to control me until he put his gun to my head and said, "I said shut up." I'd never thought that I would have a gun up to my head again. Yes, I shut up, I'm nobody's fool.

When the man cocked his gun back, I knew it was over for me. Everybody knew he had a gun looking for me, and my mom told him where I was at! My anger boiled over, but all I could do was pray.

Well, God moved, and all of a sudden there was a loud banging sound coming from the upstairs apartment and the men ran to go see what it was.

My sister, my God-sister, and I all grabbed for my baby sister and ran out the back door in the snow with no coats. We ran to a friend-of-the-family's house, I called the police and told them everything about the white boy, the guy with the gun, and where the dope was hidden. I was mad at everybody and decided everybody, including my mom, was going to pay. She sold me out; mother may I get you back for everything you allowed to happen to me.

The family friend heard me on the phone, and she said to go get my mom out the house, and try not to let the drug dealers see or hear us. We tapped on the back door, and my mom opened it. We snatched her and ran, we got to the end of the block just in time because a whole bunch of police cars pulled up in the nick of time.

After that I moved on the other side of town, I was mad at my mom and didn't want to be around her. It kept playing in my head that everybody saw this man come in the house with his gun drawn, asking for me, and I hear my mom's voice telling him where I was. Thank God again for getting me out of danger.

Chapter 12

THE CONTRACT

Shortly after that, my rap partner and I met up with two guys from New York and spent countless hours in a studio. They got us on a local talk show, and we were in a local magazine. It was nice until one day, as we were meeting, that they told us that they wanted us to stop gangster rapping and do more of a positive rap. I was not down with that.

Our name was Female Assassins and changing us would take away a lot that we had worked hard for. They wrote a positive rap for us; it was not good at all. They weren't rappers or writers. They told us we had no choice because we were on a contract. Gangster rap was all I had, it was what I took my anger out on, and it was how we won all our battles. I was not going to change.

One day I had got to a meeting late, and as I walked into the room, I could tell something was wrong from the look on Dee's face. Well, these producers found a girl from New York that would take my place. Dee was crying because she did not want to break up, but she also wanted to make it in the industry. I wanted to make it too, but not their way. We were so hurt they were going to split us up. For the sake of the group, I gave in and tried their song, I tried it their way.

One night we spent 9 hours in the studio because I could not get this song; it was not me; it was not in my heart. I was pregnant, and my feet had swollen up. We had to take a break, I went outside to get some air, and ran into one of the hottest groups in Flint, called The Dayton Family. One of the members told me they asked the managers if we could be featured on a song with them, and they were turned down. I was furious at them, first of all they turned down one of the biggest groups and didn't inform us. It was a real shot for us.

Well, that night was the last night they seen me until the loss of my baby. She was a still-born, the manager came up to the hospital and sat with me. He never brought up the contract nor either did we say anything about rap. That was neither the place nor time. Dee came to my grandmother's house after I got out the hospital. And that was the last time I saw her in years.

Chapter 13

A KNIFE TO A GUN FIGHT

I was sad after the loss of my baby girl and the split up with the group. One day we were at my friend Tasha's house, we had a few drinks and were enjoying the night. I needed that, sort of a waiting-to-exhale moment.

As always, when I'm enjoying myself, something bad always happened. This night, after all the drinking, I was tired, and my sister and I went to go lay down. Tasha had a male guest that night. They got into a heated argument, and we went to go see if she was ok. The guy (who was drunk and high) started swinging on all of us (going crazy) we all began to fight back; we beat this man with brooms, chairs and whatever else we could find.

This guy stopped in the middle of the fight and asked where was his hat? As we're standing there looking crazy and confused, he grabbed the person who was closest to him, and it was my little sister. He threw her on the sofa and reached his hand in his jacket, and said that he was going to shoot my sister.

I don't know how I got to the kitchen so fast, but I

grabbed two knives and ran back to my sister's aid. I got on this man's back and started swinging, with a knife in each hand. All the while I was swinging, I was thinking how much I hated men who hit women.

I stabbed this man in his back eight times until the blade broke off and all I had was the handle in my hand. All I knew was that I couldn't let him shoot my sister, and if he did, of course, he would have had to take all the witness.

He ran out the house and the police were called. Some people found him passed out in the snow; he didn't get too far. I didn't go to jail or serve any time. The young man lived, and he didn't press any charges. It is crazy how everybody wants to kill, but no one wants to die.

Chapter 14

SPEAK LORD, SPEAK TO ME

Two years went by, and now I'm pregnant again with my oldest son Domonique. This time I was not going to lose my baby, I prayed and asked God to give me a healthy baby. I promised to give my life back to Him. I got back into the church and was there every time the doors opened.

I moved back in with my grandmom, my mom had just got home from the hospital from having another baby. My grandmom was in the room asleep, and the baby started crying. The baby cried for a minute, my grandmom woke up and asked me to go and get the baby. I told grandmom I was sleepy, and I was not going to go and get her, her mom and dad is up there, and I rolled over and went back to sleep. As grandmom and I went back and forth for a minute with words, the baby suddenly stopped crying. I said, "See Grandma, somebody got her."

Suddenly, I heard a male's voice saying "Go and check on the baby". I knew it was the voice of the Lord (John 10: 27 says "My sheep hear my voice, and I know them, and they follow Me.") I heard His voice as clear as day, "Go and check on the baby."

I got up and walked down the hall, I could see the baby's father sitting with his arms cradled as if he was holding the baby. But as I got close to him, the baby was not in his arms. As I'm looking around for the baby, I suddenly saw little feet sticking out from under the seat cushions of the sofa. I started screaming "Get up! Get up!"

The baby was stuck in the sofa. As God helped me; I pulled my baby sister up. I was screaming for her to wake up, but she was not moving, crying or nothing, her little body was limp. Her dad was trying to get her from me because he wanted to do CPR, but it was in my spirit to pray. As we both were arguing over the baby, she's still wasn't moving. While I ran into a back room to get away from her father so that I could pray, he kept running behind me begging me to give him the baby so he could give her mouth-to-mouth.

As tears rolled down my face, I said, "Let me pray, please." My grandmother grabbed him and said, "Let her pray."

I put my heart and soul into that prayer. As she began to cry, we all screamed and shouted. Glory to God, it was Him, that was nothing but the work of God! Out of everybody in that house, God put His hands upon me that night.

Chapter 15

I'M BACK AT IT

God had blessed me with a healthy 8 lb. 7oz baby boy. For some reason the streets of Flint were not allowing me to keep my promise to God, temptation was not allowing me to keep my promise. I found myself back in the clubs, yet I was a mother now.

My son was one year old when I decided to leave everything behind and moved back to Waycross, Georgia. I found a church home and started doing Gospel poetry.

I wrote my first poem in 1999 (Soul Food, Feeding Your Soul). The Lord knew I was a nervous wreck because I was doing poetry, which was all new to me. I was not rapping and I was not in a group. The poem ended up being a hit, and they loved it, so I was back in action, I did the Gospel poetry for a couple of years before I ended back up in the streets.

One day my sister came to me and said that she had worked with a young man who was looking for a female rapper and that she gave him my number. By this time, it had been some years since I lasted rapped. She knew I didn't rap anymore and that I was not going to answer his call.

My son Domonique came up to me and said to me, "Mom, you tell me not to give up on my dreams, you should answer the man's call." So, I contacted him. We wrote two songs that he fell in love with; you could hear him playing the song a block away.

One day I was riding down Oak Street and he flagged me down, running up to the car, so happy. He explained to me that he sent the two songs to Atlanta and someone responded. He said that he was going to meet me at the house, just give him a few minutes. I waited, and about 30 minutes later my cousin called me and said that the young man was just murdered on Oak Street.

We had been planning a single releasing party, now it was a dedication party. I had to find a DJ and find another artist to perform. On my search I teamed up with two girls (Tia and Tay) and we did a song together. It was a "hit", everything came through, and it was a good show. After the show, we all agreed to become a group and called ourselves, "Female Assassins." We had hit songs and won competition after competition.

In 2006, we won the Georgia Day talent show,

singing our hit song, "Play it Raw, Lil V" featuring the Female Assassins. This competition had groups from all over, groups from Florida to Georgia, and we won. We won them all. I was ten years older than Tia and Tay, but that didn't stop these old bones. When I got that microphone in my hand, you could feel my energy. After each show, I would ask my God-sister "How did I do?" I asked because the crowd would be going crazy, but I was mentally not there. I was wherever my rap was talking about. It might have seemed like I was looking at you, but I couldn't see you.

I have been called a female 2Pac, Mystikal, Lil Wayne, and that's an honor. I was not compared to Trina or Lil Kim. See I never heard a guy stand on a street corner and quote Trina's or Kim's raps. At a show we had in Homerville, Georgia, we were performing "Play It Raw" and it was my turn to rap. As I stepped to the middle of the floor, a young man from the crowd stood in front of me; we were face-to-face and he sang my whole verse with me. That was a wonderful feeling. I remember at one competition, we were the third performers and the man stopped the show and said he didn't need to hear any more. We gave out autographs; a young man asked me to sign his chest. See, we might have not had the big riches and fame, but I had fun.

Not too long after that we broke up, due to a misunderstanding we had, and it was on my part, I take full responsibility for the split up. My heart was torn, I always thought to myself that if it was meant to be, one day we will reunite. I had moved to Valdosta, Georgia after the break-up.

In Valdosta, I decided to get my life back right with the Lord. I found a wonderful church home, I also got back into Gospel poetry and was on quite a few programs. I was in Valdosta for two years before I got a call from a young lady in Waycross to perform in a show, opening for an upcoming artist by the name of Bizzle. Of course, I refused to do the show; for one, I was back into church, and I didn't want to rap anymore. The young lady called me again. Deep in my heart I missed rap and I agreed. That weekend after the Bizzle show, I was smoking and drinking with my mom. I had to use the restroom, as I got to the bathroom, I fell to the floor, and I asked God to help me up. When I got to my feet, I saw darkness, and that's all I remembered until I could hear my mom crying. She said, "Trice baby get up, don't do this to me, get up baby." My mom said I opened my eyes, and said, "Mama I'm tired", and she said I blacked back out.

I was tired of going back and forward from Gangster Rap to Gospel. I was tired of trying to find my purpose and wonder why I was blessed with this talent and still couldn't make it in the industry. I was tired of letting God down.

My mom said it took about five more minutes before she could get me back up. She said after I went to the bathroom, she heard a big bang. She said I had blacked out and fell into her tub. I remember opening my eyes and seeing the tears rolling down my mom's face. I remember asking her "What's wrong?" She said, "Get up baby, you passed out and fell into my tub." She finally got me up and at that time my cousin called. My mom told her what happened. My cousin suggested that I go to the hospital, but I refused to go.

The next morning my cousin called and was on the three way with her friend who began to prophesy to me. She said I needed to go to the hospital now and that the Holy Spirit was telling her it was high blood pressure. I never had high blood pressure and was confused, but by her being a woman of God, I went. And as soon as I got there, they sent me straight to the back. The doctor said it was high blood pressure and that if I had not made it there in time, I would have gone into a diabetic coma!

My oh my, God is good to me! A few weeks after that, my cousin and I went out to eat, a group of young ladies were pointing at me and approached our table. One young lady asked me if I was Trice from the Female Assassins. I told her yes, she said she liked the way I rapped and walked away with her friends. I could hear her say "See, I told y'all that was her." Not even five minutes later, a man walked to my table and asked if I was Sister Monique that did the Gospel poetry, and I told him yes. My cousin and I looked at each other as if we had seen a ghost. That was crazy, and I knew at that point of my life I was living two lives, but I never did them both at the same time. Either I was in church or I was in the world.

Chapter 16

TEMPTATION AND THE BIG TEST

After living in Valdosta for three years, I found myself back in Waycross. When I left, I swore I was never moving back. After a few months of being back in Waycross, a few of the Female Assassin's fans were pressuring us to do a reunion CD. I didn't want to do it, but it felt good to be around my girls. Tia and I reconciled after five years of not speaking or rapping together. Before you know it we were back in action. My brother brought a singer to my attention; she had a little body with a big voice. Now it was four of us, three hard core rappers, and one singer.

We did Georgia Day on May 20, 2013. I was nervous. The moment we stepped on stage the crowd went wild, it was about 2,000 to 3,000 people out there, but I was uncomfortable. I thought I was ready to be back as a Gangster Rapper. I was missing something, and it was God.

I can't do this to Him anymore. I know I've been back and forward, but this time it was different.

I felt like I let God down again, and I was so

ashamed of myself. You know how that moment Adam and Eve realized that they were naked? That's how I felt, and it was not a good feeling. I felt disconnected from God. I buried myself in beer and weed, when I should have been repenting. I could feel God tugging at me. I was blinded by my talent, I thought gangster rapping was my way out of the ghetto.

One day I was at work, and I was ringing up this man's order, as I handed him his receipt, he said. "I don't know what it is that you do, but God said He needs you." As he walked away, he said, "You know what I'm talking about." I had never seen that man in my life. I tried looking for him in the restaurant, but I couldn't find him and I didn't see him leave.

I had a meeting with the group, and I let them know that I couldn't do this anymore. I wanted to go Gospel and asked the ladies to join me. We tried one song; it didn't turn out like I hoped. But they respected my decision, and that was the last time the young ladies sat at my table. That same week a Pastor walked into my restaurant and we exchanged numbers. I didn't call him or go visit his church, until one day I got a call from him and the strange thing about his call was, he called every time I was getting ready to light a blunt or on my way to go and get some weed.

It was as if God was sending him at the right time. God was sending this man to minister to me, and he did, he would hit me hard. And that's what I needed, someone who was not going to sugar coat the Gospel for me. That man had me in tears. I went to go visit the Pastor's Church (The Upper Room Outreach Ministry) and I never left.

That Pastor is still my Pastor to this day (Pastor Samuel Sellers) and I give God the Glory for my Pastor and his wife Renae Sellers, with their true hard-core teaching, no-sugar-coating ministry. God knew what He was doing when He sent them my way. A lot of people say "Every time I go to church it seemed like the Pastor's talking about me."

Has it ever occurred to you, that every time you went to church, God had a message for you? And when He wants your attention He's going to get it. The truth hurts, but stop running from the truth, because the truth also will set you free. I'm finally free, free to be me -- a woman of God, Sista Monique.

I've been tested since I've been back into church. One day I got a call from a guy saying that he was with Deff Jam, and he would like to produce The Female Assassins. He said that the rest of the group already agreed, and they were just waiting on me. When I turned him down he said that I was not going to make it because I was doing Gospel. I had him on speaker phone, I looked at my sister and smirked at her, and I told the guy no.

Satan tried to get me, but no, no, no; I'm not going back into the world anymore, I'm done. I've been rapping for 29 years, Deff Jam didn't come when I needed them, it was too late. I had repented for all my sin's, gave my life to Christ, and I was not going to turn my back on Jesus anymore. From reading this book, you know how many times Jesus saved me from being killed, and I owe Him my life. Finally, I later discovered that the guy and his record label were both scams.

Chapter 17

DYING TO BE BEAUTIFUL

I chose to put these two stories at the end of my book because these events happened throughout my life, they didn't have a certain time frame.

I was always a chubby little girl, and the food was always my friend. Before all the drinking and smoking, for me it was food. Yes, I've been called "fat" from friends, family members and others, and yes it hurt, but it did not stop me from overeating. I remember my cousin and my best friend had boyfriends and all I had was a Twinkie or a Susie Q.

One thing I could say about my best friend was that her family accepted me and my little brother. Those weekends at her house were my escape; it was my getaway from the hell I was living in. One day my friend and I went riding on Mopeds with her boyfriend and his friend. I remember being on the back of his moped with my arms wrapped around him. I thought I had me a boyfriend. These guys were racing, and my guy was losing (talking about a poor loser). My guy was fussing and asking me how much I weighed. He said, "I know my moped can go faster than this, it's you! You weigh too much." Later that night his words were playing over and over in my head. My friend asked me if I was ok; I told her I had a headache. She didn't know what the boy said and I was not going to tell her. She didn't even know my life with the beatings or nothing. Her house was my getaway, and I was not going to waste time talking about none of that mess.

After repeated thoughts of being called fat, I came up with this big idea that I would eat all the food I want and then go and make myself throw it back up. I would eat to kill the hunger but regurgitate (vomit) so the food wouldn't sit on my stomach and make me gain weight. I started to see pounds shed, and it was my little secret until I told a friend who asked how I was losing weight, then she started doing it.

One day her sister said, "Y'all are losing weight too fast, what are y'all doing to lose all that weight?" My friend told, and she started screaming and crying and saying we were going to kill ourselves; she said we could die from this. She said it was called "Bulimia". We both stopped, but I would start back to do it now and then, just to shed a few pounds. I was dying to be beautiful, maybe then someone would start loving me. Over the years, I stopped regurgitating. But right now to this day, with me trying to lose weight, the devil tries to temp me to be foolish with my body and health, but no, I will not do it.

Chapter 18

THE LORD'S TEMPLE

I have learned that my body is the Lord's temple. In this chapter I tell about how I became my own enemy. Consuming all kinds of alcohol and smoking marijuana can get the best of you, and you sometimes find yourself making a very bad decision. At the time you forget about your problems, but after that high goes down, the problems are still there.

By this time, I was catching the eyes of young men. After the weight loss, there were all these guys who wanted to talk to me. But when it came to sex, I wouldn't do it. Then all the phone calls would stop.

Life is crazy, I went through all that to get the attention, but now I got to open my legs to keep the attention? These young guys would tell me that they love me; no one had ever told me that before. No one also told me that these guys would tell you anything just to get in bed with you.

Another bad thing I started doing to the Lord's temple was sleeping with these young men, men who I wouldn't sleep with if I was sober. As I got older, I started sleeping with a deacon, married men and I'd even slept with brothers (not at the same time). One thing that stopped me from having sex was I would go and take the HIV test and pray to God "Please let the test be negative", and it would turn out negative (Thank You Jesus). This was done repeatedly, and I would hop off the table at the doctor's office and then back into the bed with a man that night. But this one time I went to go and take the HIV test and said my same prayer, but God spoke back to me: He said, "Now if you do catch it, don't blame me. I allowed for this test to come back negative, and you turn right around and lend a man your body, the Lord's Temple." That was a wake-up call. Well, that test came back negative, and I went cold turkey.

I was in the world and still not having sex. I stopped way before I gave my life back to the Lord. I realized how important my body was. I began to realize how much I disrespected the Lord's Temple; I was my own enemy. But I thank God for my wakeup call and I will not have sex until I am married and I'm patiently waiting on God. My body is the Lord's Temple.

Chapter 19

SPECIAL UPDATES

Do you remember A Preacher's Prayer? Remember the preacher who shot his wife? Well the crazy thing about that is, the woman was drunk and she went to go and pray with her children; he was sober and he also prayed. He tried to take her life, but the Grace of God saved her. She said when she heard him behind her, she turned just in time and raised her hand over her face. He shot her in the hand. I remember the doctors saying they still don't know how only her hand just got shattered. They said that with the gun he used it could have taken off her hand and her head! But she survived and he got life in prison.

Regarding my brother's father, he moved down here a few months ago and during that time, he poured his heart out to me and asked me for forgiveness, and I did forgive him. And every time we see each other now we say "I love you", we hug each other, and when I was on the program at church he was there to support me. I think God sent him here for a reason and those three months that he lived here we were closer than ever. He said he was so proud of the woman of God I became. He said, "I know your past, I know what I put you through, you was just a baby and you didn't deserve what I did to you, but you all grown up to be so strong, and I'm proud of you."

My sister recently told me that her father said every time he looks at me he sees that same little girl he hurt, but I'm not that same little girl he hurt; I am a Woman of God and I'm loving it.

Some of you might ask why forgive, but I say why not? He who angers you; controls you. Forgive in order to be forgiving. Ephesians 4:31-32 says "Let all bitterness and wrath and anger and clamor and slander be put away from you, along with all malice. Be kind to one another, tenderhearted, forgiving one another as God in Christ forgave you."

As of my mom, she is now over nine years clean. She is also married now. We had a rocky relationship, I think I was waiting on her to say she was sorry for allowing the beatings to happen to me. One day God said, "Your mom doesn't know what love is." He said, "I need you to show her the love she never had." So I forgave her and I can actually say I love her. I call her almost every day just to tell her that I love her. I hug her, I minister to her broken heart, I minister to her lost soul.

One day we were riding in the car and she began to pray. She said, "Lord, I thank You for saving my baby, I thank you for molding her into the woman of God she is, and I hope one day I could be just like her." I was amazed she prayed that.

As for me and how I'm doing: January 6, 2014 I graduated with my GED, I'm now in college as a Criminal Justice major, and I've been in college for a year now. I'm doing my internship at the Solicitor's office, working with the prosecuting attorney. I'm doing Gospel rap and poetry. I started a group with my little sister and two nieces called, "I4TL" meaning, (I'm for the Lord)

We got a hit song named "I'm for The Lord". I'm still saved and God is doing some things in my life. I'm now an Author, and this book is a dream come true. Glory be to God.

Chapter 20

CLOSING STATEMENT

Well, that's my life... The life of "Trice" on to my journey as "Sista Monique". I got one last favor to ask you all who read this. Go to your phones, IPads, or tablets and type in Donnie McClurkin and Tye Tribbett's song "We Are Victorious" and turn it up loud and sing with me.....

"We are victorious! We are victorious! Nothing can conquer us! We are victorious!"

CONTACT INFORMATION

Email Address:

flanagan.monique@yahoo.com

www.ingramcontent.com/pod-product-compliance
Lightning Source LLC
LaVergne TN
LVHW051159080426
835508LV00021B/2708